GRACE UPON GRACE

A book of devotion, purpose, and prayers

Author by
Elena Quevedo MD
Minister and Disciple

To order additional copies of this book, please contact:
Palibrio
1663 Liberty Drive
Suite 200
Bloomington, IN 47403
Toll Free from the U.S.A 877.407.5847
Toll Free from Mexico 01.800.288.2243
Toll Free from Spain 900.866.949
From other International locations +1.812.671.9757
Fax: 01.812.355.1576
orders@palibrio.com

Library of Congress Control Number: 2022900466
ISBN: Softcover   978-1-5065-3964-5
               Ebook   978-1-5065-3965-2

Print information available on the last page

Rev date: 01/14/2022

Why am I writing this book

For my love for God, I want others to love God too. Would you like to experience a love from God like never before.

Dedicated To God and My Friend David Washington

Acknowledgements

I thank my friend David Washington for the manuscripts, and giving me support and time.

Special Thanks for God for my everything

Contents

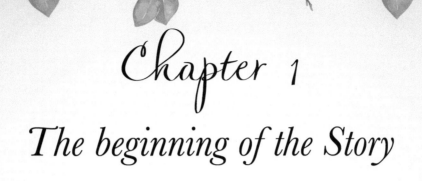

Chapter 1

The beginning of the Story

I am 70 years old, but feel and look like 40. So, I tend to attract younger men. This book is about my struggle with my bipolar and how God made it to be a condition rather than it to be a disease. Its also about love. Bipolar disease is a mood disorder, that has phases: hypomania, mania, depression, and mixed. Patients with bipolar, have great creativity. Im creative in art, and poetry. They both calm me down. The book was created to get me to open up. For all my life, I kept it inside not being able to talk about it.

I thought I was damaged goods. I was soo messed up that I couldn't cry. It became difficult for me

until I experienced Gods love. I was sexually molested by my biological father since age 9, until age 15, when the molestations stopped. My father died of colon cancer. My father developed the colon cancer which is a curse because he molested me. I never told anybody for 60 years. This was described by The Father of phycology were you will repress things for years, and it messes up your life. I was married 3 times, but the marriage failed because ever since I was molested by my father, I didn't have intimacy with my husbands. You will find that the book is very informative and it addresses common issues that a lot of people suffer from.

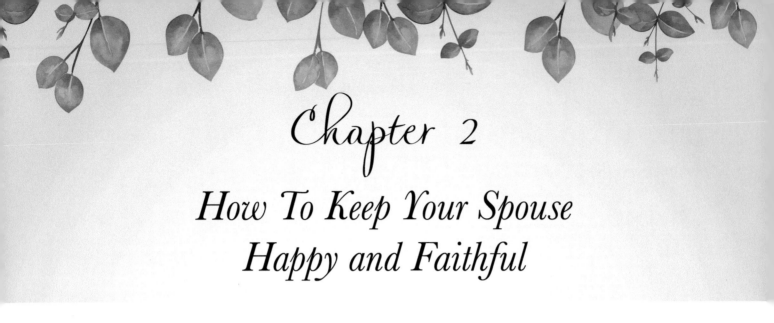

Chapter 2

How To Keep Your Spouse Happy and Faithful

For women about men, this is the way to approach your man development, sweety, your demeanor, is of a king, and you are my king, and I am your queen.

Another pick up for women, is I have never had intimacy like the one I have with you. Your love is as sweet as apples.

You and our love will blossom like the apple tree. You are my sunshine that shines only on your love and beauty.

Pick up for men to women, "You are soo beautiful that roses are envious of your great beauty."

You look at the womans eyes and you say, "your eyes are soo beautiful and transparent, that I can see that your soul is as white as snow".

Honey, I bring you these roses of love to make you soo happy. You are my diamond, that sparkles greater than all the diamonds I have ever seen in my life.

"When I walk in the house and I see you, you lit up the room as the sunshine."

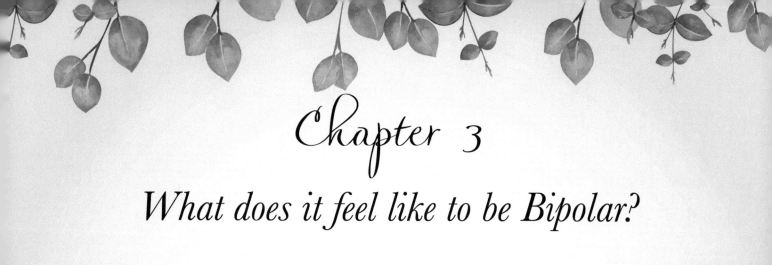

Chapter 3
What does it feel like to be Bipolar?

Bipolar is a very interesting illness. It is a diagnosis that can be hard to understand, but with great work it can be managed. The feeling of being bipolar is having 2 different types of personalities and being far different from others yet while being the same person. First, you have to think about it, people with bipolar have to take medication to deal with the illness.

Having to deal with bipolar on a daily bases can feel very overwhelming, and very stressful. Sometimes I feel I cant think right, and my ability to focus have decreased. Again, it is very manageable, but I believe with the help of God

Almighty I am able to go through this, and I pray that God does a miracle to you right now if your reading this beautiful book. Feeling anxious and sometimes difficult to deal with the reality of having bipolar is a daily challenge for those who have this sickness.

Chapter 4

Something About Me

Being the co author of this book, I am a very interesting person who has a totally different personality than other people. I am kind hearted, gentle, loving, generous, a gentlemen, patient in heart, and very hard working and faithful man. My name is David, I am the Co-author of this book. I am also a pastor that loves helping people and bring them into the beautiful hands of God.

I was raised by a mother that I dearly love. Her name is Lela Washington. Sweet, and loving mother, who's love is of that of a sweet angel. She showed and taught me how to become a kind, loving, and wonderful person that I am

today. But sadly she passed away from a brain tumor. I am diagnosed with Schizophrenia, but bipolarism is very similar to this illness. Be strong in the Lord, and be prayerful, for having these types of illnesses is not easy, and in fact, many people do not fully recover from these types of illnesses.

Chapter 5

How to Treat Your Partner

13

Its all about you, in treating your partner. The type of person you are is the type of person you will have and draw to you. A man must treat the woman he loves as his own princess teddy bear. They must have respect for there partner, and treat them with the tender love that God has for them. Show your gentle side of nature as you be with your partner, for whatever emotions or personality you have with your partner shows the type of person you really are.

If you don't have a partner, a boyfriend or a girlfriend, don't give up. There are countless people out there looking for someone special

and good like you. But sometimes you have to work and change the type of person you are to draw more attention and perhaps meet your one and true love. For example, stay looking fresh and clean, nice, and well properly dressed. But patient, ask God to give you a wife, or a loving husband if you want to be married.

Chapter 6
Bipolar and the Use of Alcohol and Drugs

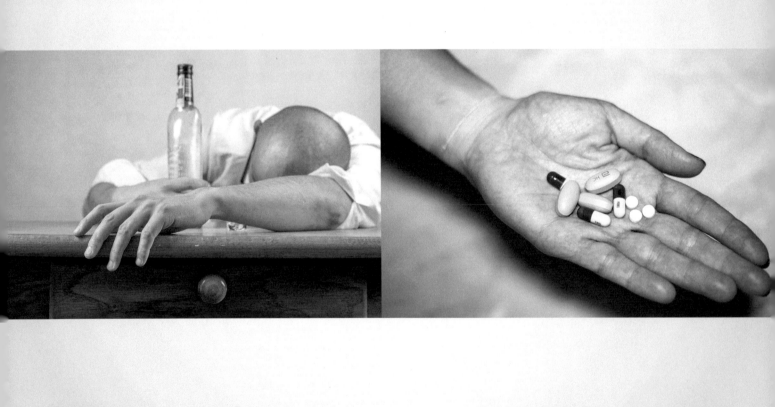

Most of the time alcohol, drugs and bipolar can lead someone totally astray from the right path, and could even lead to death. Alcohol is a bad to drink, for it is a sin and can disturb the mind and please the mind in many ways. Most car accidents are caused from alcohol and drunk driving. Now, drugs on the other hand are totally bad for the human body, and often leads to destructive consequences.

You can easily lose your life with the hand of bad drugs, but in my own opinion I call it, "The devils drug." Cocaine, meth, and other drugs can highly influence the mind and impact the human body.

For example, anyone taking these drugs often have a dead look upon there bodies, lifeless, skinny, and huge financial problems. Now with the mind, there thinking becomes twisted and deteriates the brain at a very fast pace. Just because it feels good, doesn't mean its good for you.

Chapter 7
Experience a New Life With God

God is the most beautiful person in the entire existence of life. It is your time to come in a new level with God, for God has a plan for your life. Once you lead your heart into the beautiful arms of God, he will began to make you feel special and renewed. Having an encounter with God will make you feel different, in a beautiful way, that many doors of blessings will began to fall one by one into your path.

A man cannot have 2 masters, they must decide whether they will follow God, or follow the devil. The devil wants you away from God because he knows that your life will multiply and become soo beautiful, that you will never stop worshiping and praising God for yourself. Jesus is God, the true King that every man must follow, if they want a beautiful and happy life. No one will not force you to come to God, it is your choice. But you will be missing out on a heck of a wonderful experience and a big slice of life by not allowing God to be the first in your life.

Conclusion

The Lord is our shepherd, we shall not want. He delivered us from countless situations. We have had many encounters with Satan, but the Lord that we serve have delivered us out of them all. We appreciate God in our life, for he is our blessing.

Every time we take a breath of fresh air, we appreciate the goodness of Gods unending love for us. When you face a troubled situation, call on the name of the Lord, Yashua, for he promise to save all those who call upon his holy name.

Please purchase this book since it is an extraordinary book from our hearts to yours. We hope that you will cry, laugh, and enjoy! **We need the money.**

About the Author

Elena Quevedo, medical doctor, disciple of God. Born in Panama City, Central America,

God is in my life ever since I was born. I love him dearly.

We decided to write this book to spread the word of God. This is what he want us to do.

Love your neighbor as yourself.

Thank you.

David Washington, Pastor, plumber, and Japanese translator.

Was born in Inkster, Michigan

Disciple of God

We decided to write this book to spread the word of God. This is what he want us to do.

Love your neighbor as yourself.

Thank you.

Printed in the United States
by Baker & Taylor Publisher Services